Hope for the HURTING

A Handbook for Those Experiencing Loss

Dr. Michael and Carolyn
Reynolds

Hope for the Hurting

Published 2024 by Pathway Pearls

ISBN: 979-8-9893024-0-6

Credits:
Photos are owned by the author
Cover art created in Canva

Cover Design and interior layout and editing by Alane Pearce of Pearce Writing Services, LLC. Contact at AlanePearceCoaching.com/contact.

Hope for the Hurting

Dr. Michael and Carolyn Reynolds

HOPE:

"An expectation
that things will get better."

— Michael J. Reynolds

This book is dedicated to those who are hurting:
physically, emotionally, or spiritually.

And to those people and
organizations who help them.

Words of Hope

**"Come to Me,
all you who are
weary and burdened,
and I will give you rest."
Matthew 11:28**

Table of Contents

"We are hard pressed on every side,
but not crushed;
perplexed, but not in despair;
persecuted, but not abandoned;
struck down, but not destroyed."

II Corinthians 4:8-9

A Note from the Authors

Your loss is uniquely yours. No one knows your exact situation as personally as you. Anyone who tells you, "I know how you feel" is probably wrong—well-meaning, but wrong. No one has walked in your shoes.

In times of personal loss or crisis the last thing a hurting person needs is for someone to thrust a *"Here's Help"* book in his or her face along with the well-meaning words, *"Read this, it will make things better."* The reality is that it likely won't make things better. At least not overnight.

What may be of value, however, is a concise digest of a few brief, focused, helpful points suggesting some actions, mindsets, and reframing that may offer comfort. Hurting people need to know that what they are feeling is normal, and that others have been through what they are experiencing. They need to know there are things they can do, both physically and mentally, to facilitate the healing process. And, perhaps most important of all, they need to know there is always HOPE.

Hope for the Hurting is a book of manageable doses of easily-digested hints and tips to help the grief-stricken hold on to hope. By no means is this an exhaustive essay on the subject of loss; instead this is a pocket-sized concise guidebook of likely pausing points on the way to healing. For the compassionately concerned, it is a tangible gesture of assistance. For the grief-stricken it is a valuable guide.

We pray you will be encouraged by this book.

"Blessed are they that mourn,
for they shall be comforted."
(Matthew 5:4)

**"May the God of hope
fill you with all joy and peace
as you trust in Him..."
Romans 15:13**

Words of Hope

Dealing with Loss

Loss. It's something we all deal with. It comes in all varieties of sizes and shapes, from minor annoyances all the way to life-altering tragedies. Loss can occur in virtually any area of our lives: health, job, relationships, money, family, home — you name it. No area of a person's life is immune from the potential intrusion of loss.

Turn on the news, or open the daily newspaper to see that people are dealing with loss even as you read this. Unfortunate events are quite simply a part of life, and as such, must be dealt with. Others have been where you are right now and have learned some things about loss and grief that may be of help to you. Reading a book like this is rather like receiving directions on a journey from someone who has made the trip before. They can't take the trip for you, but they can give you some directions that will make the journey smoother.

Our daughter and her family moved to Thailand as missionaries several years ago. Would you believe they even took their children, *our grandchildren,* with them? The pain of the "halfway-around-the-world" separation was huge. Our heartache motivated us to seek help from those who had long-distance grandchildren. We learned new skills—producing puppet shows on FaceTime, making talking-albums, and how to best enjoy a 26-hour flight to visit them!

It has been said that while pain is inevitable, misery is optional. When the situation is upon you, the question is not *if* I have to deal with this, but rather, *how* am I going to deal with this? Rather than remaining stuck in the miserable paralysis of grief or sadness, an intentional step in the right direction, however small, can start us on the path of healing.

As you read further, you will notice each of the chapters will suggest some concrete steps that someone experiencing loss could take. These brief chapters will present some intentional actions that can help move you forward in the process of healing your hurt.

Our hope is that the pages of this book will help put things in a perspective that will make your journey a bit easier. Our hope is that this book will help you realize you are stronger than you thought.

Personal Reflections

Your world has been turned upside down. What are some aspects of your life that have remained relatively stable?

When you suffered loss in the past, what has helped?

What do you think would be one positive thing that may lessen your hurt right now?

Heavenly Father,
I ask for Your wisdom and comfort
during this season of loss.
Amen

"The Lord is close to the brokenhearted..."
Psalm 34:18

Overcoming Grief

Grief is not only natural; it's necessary.

While the word "grief" is a noun describing a condition or an emotional place in which we find ourselves, the word "grieve" is a verb, which means it's calling for action. Grief is something you *experience*; grieving is something you *do*. And it's okay to do it. In fact, it's important to your overall emotional health and healing that you allow the grieving process to take place. God designed it as part of the process of restoration following a loss in our lives. It's not only natural, but it's necessary.

Crying, shouting, anger, sadness, sleeplessness— the grieving process is different for each of us. But it is an active journey each of us must take as we experience loss. A well-known psychologist, Dr. Elisabeth Kubler-Ross, described grief as a 5-stage progression:

- **DENIAL** is a defense mechanism whereby a person refuses to fully accept the fact that a loss event has occurred. It is a natural response to a painful intrusion that is simply too much to deal with initially.
- **ANGER** is an emotional response to a loss event whereby the person experiencing it is just plain mad at the world, and oftentimes directs that anger to those closest to them.

- **BARGAINING** is a stage in the grief process whereby the person suffering loss attempts to mitigate the pain by "striking a deal" with the other person, entity, or even God in hopes of lessening the impact, or to reverse the loss.
- **DEPRESSION** can occur when the loss recipient realizes that the event is real and possibly irreversible. In the stark light of reality, a deep sadness can ensue.
- **ACCEPTANCE** occurs when the inevitability of the loss is fully realized, and the person can now face what is next with a degree of objectivity.

Admittedly this is a man-made matrix designed to describe a God-given healing process, and as such is not a sequence that is set in stone. Its value is that it describes some of the emotions we are likely to experience as we pass through the valley of grief. We may experience some or all of these emotions and not necessarily in that order. These feelings are common during seasons of grief.

In the beloved Psalm 23, the writer (David) tells us, "...though I walk through the valley of the shadow of death, I will fear no evil, for Thou art with me..." Notice David uses the word "*through*" as he describes the passage among the dark days.

He didn't use the word "stay" or "camp out" in the valley. It may be a tough trek, and certainly one we may not have chosen. But grief is a journey we've been given, and it ultimately has an exit. You will get through this.

Grief is not only natural, it's necessary.

Personal Reflections

Why is it important to "vent" what you're feeling now?

Who is someone you could contact so you could share your heart?

How can you express to God how you feel?

Father God,
Wrap me in your loving arms as You lead me through this time of grief.
I need your healing.
Amen

"Never will I leave you, never will I forsake you "
Hebrews 13:5

Words of Hope

God's Perspective

God sees the end from the beginning, and we don't.

It's important for us to keep in mind that God's perspective on our circumstances is different from ours; *way different*. He truly has the big picture, while we only see the small segment that immediately surrounds us. In no way minimizing what we may be experiencing, it may well be a minuscule segment of a greater tapestry that is beyond our capacity to visualize at this point. We can only see a tiny skewed portion of a much larger magnificent design.

Is there a lesson for us to learn?

Is this part of God's curriculum for us?

What might He be teaching us here?

Our Old Testament friend, Isaiah, put it this way:

> *"For My thoughts are not your thoughts, neither are My ways your ways," declares the Lord. "As the heavens are higher than the earth, so are My ways higher than your ways, and My thoughts than your thoughts." (Isaiah 55:8-9)*

Simply put, God sees the end from the beginning, and we don't.

Consider one of those 1000-piece jigsaw puzzles that display a beautiful scene on the outside of the box. We are all aware of the confusing complexity of pieces that lies inside that same box. While God sees the completed project, our circumstances may feel like the single perplexing piece of the puzzle that we hold in our hands right now. Maybe there's more to this than what we see. Things are simply too fresh to appreciate the final picture. The pieces are too jumbled to visualize the completed portrait.

As time passes, and more of the puzzle falls into place, we begin to get a sense of the bigger picture, the larger perspective: God's perspective.

Personal Reflections

God has said, "*Never will I leave you, never will I forsake you.*" *Hebrews 13:5*

How have you seen God's presence, even in your grief and in the midst of your questions?

How does knowing God will never leave you bring you comfort?

During this difficult time of uncertainty, what or who has brought you comfort?

Creator God,
Enable me to trust Your plan for my life.
Help me to understand Your perspective.
Amen

"Be strong and take heart all you who hope in the Lord."
Psalm 31:24

There's Always Hope

You can hold on to hope.

Depending on the particular circumstance, things may look pretty bleak. Life can be brutal at times and the situation is seemingly hopeless.

However, not to minimize frivolously what people sometimes have to face, for believers there's always hope. We can look ahead to the "other side" of the situation. That other side may be obscured or totally unimaginable at the moment but be assured it is there. Remember that loss and grief is a journey, not a destination. Whatever you do, don't give up hope.

The Bible tells us in the book of Galatians not to become weary and not give up. Galatians 6:9 says, "Let us not become weary in doing good, for at the proper time we will reap a harvest if we do not give up."

Easier said than done, to be sure, but the point is to hang in there and know things will get better. When we've taken a hit, we mustn't let it sink the ship, no matter how bad it seems at the time. We may have to limp along at half speed for a while as healing and restoration begin to take place, but the point is to keep moving.

Isaiah, the Old Testament Prophet, gave us these words of encouragement: "But those who hope in the Lord will renew their strength. They will soar on wings like eagles; they will run and not grow weary, they will walk and not grow faint" (Isaiah 40:31).

And Jesus in the New Testament book of John echoes the same words of hope to us when He said, "In this world you will have trouble. But take heart! I have overcome the world" (John 16:33). These are biblical lifelines we can cling to during the tough times.

Winston Churchill, while not a biblical prophet, was nonetheless a man of great wisdom and encouragement as he led Great Britain through some of the darkest days of World War II. In the face of the horrors of the incessant German bombing attacks and the prediction of an imminent invasion, Churchill exhorted his fellow countrymen with the following words: "Never give in" (to the darkness). "Never, never, never, never give in." His words ring true today. Never give in to the darkness of your circumstances and never give up. The Brits never gave up and ultimately won the victory, and so will you.

Reflections

It has been said that one of the most potent antidotes to sadness is to consider the things for which we can still be thankful.

Even in this season, can you name three things for which you are thankful?

1.

2.

3.

How do Bible verses like these give you hope?

"Be joyful in hope, Patient in affliction, Faithful in prayer."
Romans 12:12

"But those who hope in the Lord will renew their strength..."
Isaiah 40:31

God of Hope,
Thank You for your unfailing love for me. You are my source of comfort, strength, and hope.
Amen

Words of Hope

"...weeping may stay for the night, but rejoicing comes in the morning."
– Psalm 30:5

Get Up and Make Your Bed

It's time to make yourself get moving.

Say what? Nobody's told me to make my bed since I was in middle school! What's that got to do with anything? Good question.

When you've taken a hit, it's easy to slip into a serious case of the "blahs". You think, "What's the use? I don't feel like doing much of anything." You feel like the wind has been taken out of your sails, and in many ways it has. But just like in a boat when the wind dies, you have to pick up the oars, start rowing, and get the ship moving again. Take action.

Better said, it's time to make yourself get moving, no matter how bad you feel. It cuts against human nature, because (as we've said before), when you're hurt you want to hide and pull the covers over your head. It's so easy to just let things go.

Though not easy, you've got to pull the covers off, get up, and make your bed. Get moving. Put your head down, put one foot in front of the other, and force yourself to get in motion. Straighten up your room. Do your laundry, take a walk. Go to the gym.

Watch "Jeopardy" (while you're jogging in place, of course). Movement and intentional activities get the blood flowing, release certain positivity-inducing chemicals in your body, and help buy you time (which is our ally). You'll feel better if you move.

You recall how it is when you ride a bicycle. First you have to get on, but it's no good to you until you start peddling. If you just sit on it, you'll topple over; but when you start pumping the pedals, then you can go somewhere. But you have to start moving.

And that starts when you get up and make your bed.

"As the rain and the snow come down from heaven, and do not return to it without watering the earth and making it bud and flourish, so that it yields seed for the sower and bread for the eater, so is my word that goes out from my mouth: It will not return to me empty, but will accomplish what I desire and achieve the purpose for which I sent it."
(Isaiah 55:10-11)

Reflections

It's easy to stay stuck when you are down. Consider some things that make you feel calm and relaxed. Write your thoughts.

1. Music

2. Location

3. Friend

4. Activity

5. Food

Kind Father,
Help me trust that You have a plan for each day of my life. Please show me Your path for me today.
Amen

"For where two or three are
gathered in my name,
I am there."
Matthew 18:20

Call a Friend or Two

Special situations call for extraordinary responses.

The military has a term for it: Special Ops. Ask yourself, "Who could I call at 2:00 o'clock in the morning and ask for prayer? Who are the two or three people in my life that are my absolute A-Team prayer partners?" We're talking warriors here: Army Rangers, Navy Seals, the Marines. Those people in your life who will take your situation seriously and go into fully-committed prayer warfare on your behalf. Sound a little radical? It is. Serious situations call for serious support. You're in a tough spot and you need the people who care about you most to step up and go to God on your behalf.

If you don't have an A-Team in place, there is still help available. Organizations such as local churches, Samaritan's Purse, and Salvation Army have resources in place to help.

People want to help. How many times during a time of loss have we heard someone say, "Is there anything I can do...?"

Consider specific ways others can be of help. Get your trusty pen and number 1-5.

1. What is one thing you need to do in the next hour?

2. What would be helpful today (run errand, pick up children, mow lawn)?

3. Organize meals.

4. Office work.

5. List an "out-of-the-box" item you might enjoy (a Book, DVD, etc.)

These well-meaning friends truly desire to render assistance, but just don't know what to say, or what to do. Now you have a few suggestions, and it's a sincere response to a sincere outreach. Give them specifics.

Let's face it. You can only consume so many tuna casseroles. Specific, serious, sincere prayer is a privilege for those who pray, and a blessing for whom the prayers are uttered. Your own prayers, and those lifted up on your behalf will take you a lot further on your journey to healing than just cookies and casseroles. Of course, never turn down cookies. Let's not be foolish here.

Assemble your strike force and turn them loose in prayer. You need them, and there are those who want to do something tangible to help ease your burden.

It may take courage to reach out to others, but you can do it! Someone is waiting for your call.

Reflections

Who are some friends you could call for support and encouragement? Write their names and numbers here.

1.

2.

3.

Next time you are alone and wish you had someone to talk to, call someone on the list above.

Also remember God is right there beside you. How can you remind yourself of his presence?

Gracious God,
Bless my faithful friends,
and help me to be a faithful friend to others.
Thank You, Jesus, for being my
eternal companion.
Amen

Words of Hope

"Finally, brothers and sisters, whatever is true, whatever is noble, whatever is right, whatever is pure, whatever is lovely, whatever is admirable—if anything is excellent or praiseworthy—think about such things."

Philippians 4:8

Social Distancing

We need the support and encouragement of others.

During the COVID Pandemic, one of the buzz words that reverberated throughout its course was "social distancing." The Centers for Disease Control set forth this concept as being one of the keys to slowing the spread of the disease. Simply put, it was a way to describe the importance of remaining a safe physical distance from others. Social distancing provided enough space between us to make transmission of the disease less likely. It turned out to be an incredibly simple yet effective way of slowing the spread.

As important as maintaining a physical distance was during the pandemic, we also realized the importance of sustaining a social or relational connectedness. Many of us continued contact with others via phone calls, Zoom, and online chats.

During this period of national distress, the value of personal or social connectedness became vividly apparent.

The same need applies when we find ourselves in seasons of personal crisis. We need the support and encouragement of others during our times of setback and loss. The tendency, however, is to withdraw into our own woundedness, while what we need is just the opposite: to stay connected.

Stay connected to people. Positive people are often a great source of comfort and encouragement. People who care for you are the ones who will walk with you through the mess. Even if you're not all that lovable right now, there are people in your life who will love you anyway.

Stay connected to God. If you are a person who prays, now is the time to pick up the pace. Even if you are angry or are simply at a loss as to why something has happened, God wants to hear from you. You and I are His kids, and a parent loves nothing more than to hear from His children. God is like other fathers in that regard. If you're not normally a praying person, now might be a good time to begin a conversation with God. Just talk to Him as you would a friend. Pour out your heart to Him including your disappointment, anger, and pain. Cry out to Him!

Stay connected to God's Word, the Bible. The Bible is a huge source of comfort and wisdom in times of distress. The book of Psalms has proven to be especially comforting to many. As God spoke words of truth, support, and encouragement through the Bible writers, He speaks those same words into your situation as you read His Word. And He promises it is never a fruitless endeavor.

Social distancing may be effective during a pandemic, but staying socially connected during periods of personal loss is an essential component of the healing process.

Stay connected to God's Word
Stay connected to people
Stay connected to God

Reflections

What are some ways you can stay connected to others even at a distance?

If you don't feel like reading your Bible during this time, pick your favorite verse and say it over and over again. Use the space below to write it down. Keep your God connection.

Many people send cards during times of grief. Save your cards and reread them occasionally.

Loving Father,
Thank You for the people You have brought into my life. May our relationships be a blessing to one another.
Amen

"Don't worry about anything, but pray about everything; tell God your needs and don't forget to thank him for his answers. And the peace of God shall guard your heart and your mind. Finally, whatever is true...lovely think on these things."

Philippians 4:6-8 (paraphrased)

Words of Hope

Control Your Thoughts

Take your thought life captive.

Negative thoughts are a natural companion to negative experiences. They go hand in hand with loss, but they are a hand that will drag you down and make a bad situation even worse. Consider the last time you had a serious car break-down, or maybe even an accident. Our thoughts are consumed by all the negative components of an auto malfunction.

Or how about a job furlough or layoff? Of course our minds churn over all the ways our lives will be impacted by such a significant turn of events.

Sour thoughts can take you on a dark, downward spiral at a time you need just the opposite. The tendency for many is to accelerate the spiral by dwelling on the worse case scenarios that may result from whatever has gone wrong. Unfortunately, vain speculation such as this usually makes things worse. This is a time when some active re-framing and thought redirection can be of great benefit.

What can you do when you feel your thoughts taking a downturn? The New Testament book of 2 Corinthians gives us a useful technique that can help us through those times when our neurons turn negative. "*Take every thought captive in obedience to Christ.*" (2 Corinthians 10:5) It's simply a reminder that we possess at least a degree of control over our thoughts. It's an intentional intervention where we shut off the negativity and shift to something else.

When bad things happen, there is a tendency to play the blame-shame-mind game. We blame others, or ourselves, sometimes even God, for our circumstance. If our thoughts run unchecked, they spiral downward resulting in negative emotions such as bitterness, self-pity, or anger. Blaming is generally a fool's errand and rarely does anything good come of it. Choosing to think positively, we use thought control to realize that forgiveness is a critical step toward healing. Sometimes it is necessary to forgive others, even if you were in the right. Sometimes it's important to forgive yourself. Hey, life happens, and we need not live in self-condemnation.

Think of your television remote. If you don't like what you're watching, you pick up the remote and change channels. You're in control. You've taken the television captive, not vice versa.

Granted, changing a thought direction may not be as easy as changing channels on a television, but it is possible to stop the downward mental spiral by switching from the hurt to the happy in your mind. Switch to the vacation channel, or the grandchildren channel, or the bass fishing channel, or an inspirational channel. Whatever it is, stop watching channel sad, and hit the mental button to something else. Take your thought life captive. The reception is so much better when you do.

Reflections

When you find yourself worrying, uplifting music can often soothe your soul. Soft praise or classical music can be calming.

List some other activities that are calming for you. Then refer to this list when you feel overcome by your thoughts.

When you are tormented with negative thoughts or memories, consider saying to yourself "STOP!" Reframe those thoughts with a positive statement or Scripture. It may be helpful to keep a 3x5 card in your pocket with the word "STOP" one side, and a positive saying on the other side.

List some positive sayings you could put on the back of that reminder card:

God of Compassion,
Help me not be consumed by the thoughts and worries of this world. Transform and renew my mind according to Your will.
Amen

"For I know the plans I have for you," declares the Lord, "plans to prosper you and not to harm you, plans to give you hope and a future."
Jeremiah 29:11

Go Figure

Actually, don't.

Don't try to make sense of everything that happens. In this world, sometimes stuff just happens, and trying to figure out the "why" will leave you with more questions than answers. Dwelling on why an event has taken place in our lives can get us stuck on trying to figure it out and in the process delay our healing.

Well-meaning friends may attempt to provide comfort by reciting worn clichés that don't hold much meaning at this point. "Everything happens for a reason," or "they're in a better place." Sometimes friends just don't know what to say, and that's when these platitudes are recited. It probably makes them feel better, but not necessarily the one who is hurting.

The "why" may or may not come later. God may favor us with an explanation at some point in the future, and we get a glimpse of the bigger picture.

Often a purpose or a plan to what we're going through may be shrouded at the moment. Focusing on the why can take our eyes off the goal of physical and emotional restoration. Better to allow the why to come to you than pursue it at a time better suited to other areas of healing.

The good news is that God can take a bad situation and make something positive out of it. We live in a world where unfortunate things happen, but that's where our faith in God's ultimate goodness comes in. Not our faith in our ability to figure it out.

For now, our focus must be to lean on our faith and lean into the next hours and days ahead of us. Go figure? Not now.

Reflections

List anything positive you can see coming out of your present situation:

Write a note telling God just how you feel and where you would like to see yourself in the future. Realize that you are a work in progress and the steps toward your new goals could be very small ones.

All-Wise God,
Even when I don't understand the "whys" of my life, help me trust in You and not lean on my own understanding.
Amen

Words of Hope

"Cast all your anxiety on Him (God), because He cares for you."
1 Peter 5:7

Avoid the Three "D's"

Just Say No!

Several years ago a campaign was instituted to discourage substance abuse: "Just say No!" Its purpose was to encourage people to be intentional in their rejection of a bad choice. In the face of a loss in our lives, there are three "Despicable D's" that we would do well to say "no" to.

The first is to define. When hurt in our lives seems so overwhelming, our tendency is to allow that event to define who we are. Consider your life before your loss: for better or worse, that was the genuine you. When a major hit happens, the tendency is to allow that event to disproportionately define who we are. Is this event a major disruption in your life? Of course, it is. But does it define who you are from now on? Not necessarily. Allowing a negative episode in our life story define who we are is seldom productive. ***Just say No!***

There was more to you before your change-point event, and there will be the same you as you adapt to unfamiliar thoughts, feelings, or circumstances. Yes, you may reconstruct your exterior environment, and reinvent your interior self, but the real you is still alive and has purpose. Is this event a major hit in your life? Of course. Does it define you? Absolutely not. Don't let this thing define you. ***Just say No!***

Second, this must not be allowed to divide you from others. Most of us have others in our lives who are also affected by this event. At a time when it's important to circle the wagons and draw together, the tendency is to allow our sadness to divide us. Our own woundedness can cause us to say unkind words and withdraw into our own hurts. That's the worst possible place to be. Solomon, a pretty smart guy, writes in the Old Testament book of Ecclesiastes, "*Two are better than one…If one falls down, his friend can help him up. But pity the man who falls and has no one to help him up.*" (Ecclesiastes 4:9-10) Don't let this thing divide you. ***Just say No!***

And finally, remember that our age-old enemy, Satan, has declared his game plan in the New Testament book of John: "*…the thief comes only to steal and kill and destroy…*" (John 10:10). But Jesus promises us in that same verse, "*I have come that they may have life, and have it to the full.*" Don't let this season of your life destroy you.

Define—Divide—Destroy: ***Just say No!***

Reflections

Let's think about the real you. What defines you?

What are three things you would consider your strengths?

Which of these strengths are operating for you now?

Gracious Lord,
Remind me that my life is defined by You,
and not the world around me.
Your love for me is amazing.
Amen

"…His (God's) compassions never fail, they are new every morning. Great is your faithfulness."
Lamentations 3:22-23

Let Time Be Your Friend

The Tincture of Time.

You might be familiar with the old adage: "Time heals all wounds." The idea here is that the passage of time has the tendency to soften a blow, or to take the edge off the pain. The medical profession even has a term for the concept. Back in the old days, doctors used to refer to it as the *"tincture of time."* Many aches and pains, if given a little time, will get feeling better. It's not always the best treatment, but there's some truth to the concept.

In medicine, the passage of time allows the healing process to gradually lessen the pain. Such is often the case when we have suffered a painful event in our lives. While time may not change our circumstance, it does give us the opportunity to process the event and put it into life's larger perspective.

Time is God's way of allowing us to heal emotionally, physically, and spiritually. Does it make the circumstance go away? No. Does time negate the need for mending and restoration? No. What time gives us is hope. Time gives us the hope things will get better and the pain we are now experiencing will diminish. Gradually you may begin to notice a new perspective as you progress toward your new normal.

Time is our ally in the face of loss. We can't speed it up or accelerate the process, and certainly progress is difficult to detect on an hourly or daily basis.

But things will look better a month from now or a year from now. Even in our own past, we can look back at tough times and confirm that the passage of time has helped soften what was once intense pain. We already have a "track record" in this area. That gives us hope, and hope is a huge part of the healing process. So take your time. Breathe.

Overnight, things don't often get better, but time will soften pain. Time is a subtle, yet effective, healer.

Reflections

How would you like things to look a year from now?

What would give you hope?

What would be the first step you could take to get you moving toward your new goal?

Eternal Father,
Help me be steadfast in my faith.
Your Word tells me the sufferings of this present world cannot compare
to the glory to be revealed one day.
Amen

"He (God) heals the brokenhearted and binds up their wounds."
Psalm 147:3

Be a Wounded Healer

Someone needs your experience.

One of our favorite movies is "Forrest Gump." If you've seen it, you're already grinning as you recall some of the memorable scenes from the improbable life story of the young man from Greenbow, Alabama, portrayed by the inimitable Tom Hanks. You may recall a segment when Forrest was a soldier in Viet Nam, caught in an ambush and shelling from the enemy. As the scene progressed, Forrest was wounded.

However, in spite of his own wounds, he repeatedly ventured back into the holocaust of napalm to retrieve several of his fallen comrades. For his uncommon valor, he deservedly received the Congressional Medal of Honor. Somehow Forrest was able to look past his own woundedness and see that others around him were hurting even more than himself, and he forced himself to go to their aid even at his own peril. Forrest Gump, among many other things, was a wounded healer.

Far from easy, as we survey the territory around us from our vantage point of loss, we needn't look far before we spot a fellow traveler who has taken a hit just as we have. It may be a similar injury or a wound quite different from ours. But suffice it to say that hurting people intersect our lives daily.

One of the great accelerators of healing in our own instance is to reach out with a word or deed of encouragement to another who is hurting. It can serve as a huge boost to both the recipient and the donor. It helps you focus on someone else's hurt, and de-focus on yours. Something you have learned on your journey of healing can touch the heart of someone who needs the words only you can give.

The New Testament book of 2 Corinthians gives us a biblical perspective on this process when it tells us *"He (God) brings us alongside someone else who is going through hard times so that we can be there for that person just as God was there for us."* (2 Corinthians 1:3-4)

Forrest Gump was certainly no preacher or even a clinical psychologist, but he summed it up in another great line from the movie: "I'm not a smart man, but I know what love is." Forrest demonstrated that love on a terrible day in Viet Nam when he showed us how to be a wounded healer.

Reflections

Has someone done something nice for you lately? What was it? What did it mean to you?

How do you think it may be helpful for you to focus on the needs of others?

Does anyone come to mind who could use a word of encouragement from you? Write his or her name here and make an effort to reach out to them today.

Healing Father,
Help me be sensitive to the hurts in others,
and to reach out even as You are healing me.
Amen

"Rescue me and deliver me out of mighty waters…"
Psalm 144:7

Start a Journal

Write it down.

Whether it's a good joke, an amusing anecdote, or a pearl of wisdom—these days if we don't write it down, it's gone. Gone like a deleted e-mail, a lost sock, or the gift card you thought still had money on it. Things you thought could be retrieved from your cerebral hard drive can sometimes vanish. Keeping a journal of some kind can help you revisit some thoughts, principles, and helpful ideas of therapeutic value in the healing process. It's a way of cataloging some pearls of wisdom so you can refer back to them in moments when you need reminding of just how far you've come, and how you got there.

We're not talking about a daily diary here, although for some that might be a good fit. Rather, the informal writing would be a place to record the words of encouragement you received from a friend. It might include some profound words of wisdom from someone who has been right where you are now—and survived. It would chronicle the verses and passages from the Bible that God put there just for you at this specific point in your life. We've cited a few verses from the Bible in some of the previous sections. Remember Psalm 23? God gave those comforting and encouraging words to David during a particularly dark time in his life. He recorded them, and they have been an incredible source of solace to countless hurting travelers for over 3,000 years.

Your Journal of Hope may not endure quite that long, but it may help you get through tonight. It may help get someone else through a dark night as well. Write it down.

***Your Journal of Hope...
may help get someone else
through a dark night.***

Reflections

There is no right or wrong way to journal.

Probably the simplest way to journal is to use a notebook and express your thoughts and feelings in writing. Often journaling takes the form of writing letters to oneself, God, or others. However, you may be as creative as you like.

Journaling can help you realize options, help you form a plan of action, and help you visualize a path toward your new normal. It can help you realize that you have renewed strength to endure, courage to overcome, and faith to persevere.

Take pen and paper, and just get started writing. Just as David wrote in the Psalms as his heart cried out to God for deliverance from his circumstances, so you too can cry out for deliverance. Be prepared with a box of tissues to allow hope to replace your hurting heart.

You will be amazed at what you learn as you write.

Personal Thoughts:

Dear God,
Help my thoughts be conformed to your will,
and to remember how far you've brought me.
Amen

Words of Hope

"But blessed is the one who trusts in the LORD, whose confidence is in him. They will be like a tree planted by the water that sends out its roots by the stream. It does not fear when heat comes; its leaves are always green. It has no worries in a year of drought and never fails to bear fruit"
Jeremiah 17:7-8

Your New Normal

New normal holds the promise of a better day.

In many instances following loss, the aftermath of your world looks very different from the way things were before. Sometimes the difference is subtle, but often the changes in our physical, emotional, or spiritual environment are significant. Things will be different on the "other side" of a life-changing event. Moments of sadness may recur. Yearning for the normalcy of the way things were, we rarely return to the routines of our former life. When life adjusts to your present circumstances, it has been called the "New Normal" with new routines, new coping skills, possibly new settings and maybe new relationships.

Change is often a stressful process. Even positive changes such as a job promotion, or a new baby, result in a new level of stress. But when negative change occurs, oh my, stress multiplies! Our tendency is to long for the days of predictability and familiar routines and people. Change can be unsettling and sometimes frightening. But change can bring about positive outcomes as well.

Recently I spied a plaque which resounded in my heart:

When something bad happens
You can let it define you,
You can let it destroy you,
or
You can let it strengthen you.

When we look back on our lives and consider some of the major change-points, many were changes for the good. There have certainly been other times of new normals in your past which resulted in a new positive direction. Perhaps when you left home for school, marriage, or a new job?

This present season of change has the potential to bring about a new, positive normalcy; different, but better. Take the challenge of the plaque and allow your hurtful experience to strengthen you.

Consider poor Joseph from the Bible. You know the one with the colorful coat?

His brothers threw him into a pit and temporarily left him for dead. They reconsidered and decided instead to sell him to a caravan of traders.

Talk about a serious life-changing experience! Years later, because of Joseph's faithful diligence, his new normal resulted in a high position in the royal court of the Egyptian dynasty where he effectively ran the county.

Joseph is later quoted as he addresses his contrite brothers, *"You meant it for evil, but God meant it for good."* (Genesis 50:20)

That potential exists for you.

New normal is seldom easy. But it holds the promise of a better day. A day not to be feared but anticipated with hope that today's hurt will develop into tomorrow's victory.

New normal is seldom easy. But it holds the promise of a better day.

Reflections

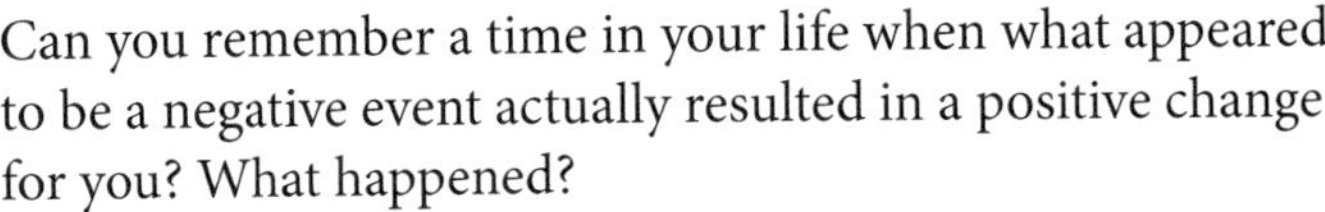

Can you remember a time in your life when what appeared to be a negative event actually resulted in a positive change for you? What happened?

What might your "new normal" look like?

What seems hardest about "new normal"? How can you overcome that challenge?

Dear God of New Beginnings,
Help me embrace my "New Normal" and see with a new vision of hope. I need your guidance as I walk this uncharted path.
Amen

"Be still, and know that I am God..."
Psalm 46:10

Planting New Dreams

God is a God of new life.

We end with a concept that at first may seem a bit far-fetched. Is it possible that your present situation is not so much an end point as it is a change point? Is this the place where you begin to look beyond the present set of circumstances and see a new direction, one you have never before considered? Admittedly, some situations are so utterly disruptive that the thought of there being a "what's next?" seems remote. In no way are we attempting to trivialize what may be a devastating season of hurt or loss.

But consider stories we have all heard, stories of incredibly harsh events in the lives of others that have somehow resulted in a totally unexpected change of direction which yielded unimaginable blessing to the person affected. You can probably even recall an event or two in your own life where what appeared to be a bad thing actually turned out to be just the opposite. You can look back and see the good that came out of what may have appeared to be hopelessly dark at the time.

Often from the dark soil of sorrow new dreams, new hopes, and new beginnings germinate and begin to form. What new direction may be coming into focus? What new season of hope and optimism may be about to spring forth? Perhaps now is the time to begin to consider the new dreams and new direction that may be on the other side of this present season of loss.

Each Easter we celebrate the resurrection of Jesus Christ. Although it is at the very heart of the Christian faith, it is an event commemorated annually by believers and non-believers alike. But think with us for a moment what actually transpired during that fateful week in Jerusalem 2,000 years ago.

Jesus Christ, the God-given and prophetically-predicted Messiah, entered the Holy City at the pinnacle of popularity. He was hailed by the masses as His processional wound through the city streets on what we now call Palm Sunday. His followers were elated and hopeful. And yet less than a week later He hung dead on a Roman cross, the apparent victim of a vicious conspiracy and an even more vicious death at the hands of His Caesarean captors. Hopes were dashed as His bewildered followers scattered for their very lives. Devastation and despair likely cannot begin to describe what was consuming their every fiber during the next three days. Hope and optimism were but distant memories.

And then came Easter morning. You know the story. The tomb was empty and what Jesus had told them all along He would do—He did. He had conquered death. Not only for Himself, but for everyone who would believe in Him. *"For God so loved the world that he gave his one and only Son, that whoever believes in him shall not perish but have eternal life."* (John 3:16)

From the incomprehensible darkness of the crucifixion sprang forth the equally incomprehensible glory of the resurrection. From the dark soil of sadness there arose a new era of life and hope.

God is a God of new life, new hopes, new dreams, new directions. As we look to Him as our true source and sustainer, we can have confidence that He will see us through this present season of challenge and reveal to us His plan for the next chapter of our lives. Therein lies the ultimate source of hope for our future.

Reflections

Perhaps it is time to allow yourself to throw off the old and put on the new! New goals that revive your heart, make you smile, lighten your step, and cause you to look forward to getting up each day…to find new hope and joy in your journey!

Where can you go to feel the presence of God?

Write in your journal your thoughts regarding your new dreams.

Precious Jesus,
I pray that somehow through the loss and hurt I have experienced, ETERNAL BLESSINGS will blossom forth in TRIUMPH, to YOUR GLORY!
Amen

**"...but those who hope in the Lord
will renew their strength.
They will soar on wings like eagles;
they will run and not grow weary,
they will walk and not be faint."
Isaiah 40:31**

Words of Hope

EPILOGUE:

The Missing "Peace"

When all is said and done, the thing we seek most in the midst of our season of hurt and loss, is a sense of peace. It is a peace that springs from the assurance that in spite of all going on in us, or around us, there is a God who loves us and offers us the certainty of an eternity in heaven with Him. With that assurance in mind, everything happening in our lives can be seen in such a much larger perspective:

an ETERNAL perspective.

How do we find this peace that is often so elusive in our broken world? The Bible offers us a simple, yet profound pathway to the ultimate peace:

PEACE with God.

First, the Bible tells us that our Creator, God, loves all the world with an unfailing love and desires that we spend eternity in heaven with Him. (John 3:16)

Second, the Bible makes it clear that we cannot "earn" our way into heaven with good deeds. It states that each person is born with an imperfect nature which the Bible calls sin. (Romans 3:23)

Third, the Bible tells us that God sent His son, Jesus, to come to the earth and satisfy the requirement of entry into heaven when Jesus died on the cross in Jerusalem 2000 years ago. This is what we celebrate at Easter. (John 3:16) & (John 14:6)

And finally, God extends this invitation to all mankind, but leaves the choice up to each person to BELIEVE AND RECEIVE JESUS through a simple heartfelt prayer. By faith, we can either embrace and accept this free gift of peace and eternity, or not. (Romans 10:8-9)

This "missing peace" is peace with God. And it comes through our faith in God, and His son, Jesus Christ. With that peace as our eternal assurance, we truly can experience "Hope for the Hurting."

Take Care of Yourself: Personal Checklist – Basics

Take time. . .

Physically:
- Nutrition – eat well, stay hydrated
- Exercise – be as active as you can
- Sleep – rest is critical

Emotionally:
- Connect with others – reach out
- Choose to look on the "bright side"
- Practice forgiveness

Spiritually:
- Trust in God to move you forward
- Read uplifting books
- Listen to praise music

"Blessed be the God and Father of our Lord Jesus Christ, the Father of mercies and God of all comfort, who comforts us in all our tribulation, that we may be able to comfort those who are in any trouble, with the comfort with which we ourselves are comforted by God."

2 Corinthians 1:3-4

Acknowledgments

As we have traveled our pathway in life, there have been many who have paved the way before us. It has been our heart's desire to share HOPE for those who are hurting, and to live a purposeful life leaving a legacy of faithful footprints.

First, we want to thank God for His grace in gifting us with a Christian heritage and faithful parents: Mary and Edward Hensley, and Audrey and Stanley Reynolds.

We are so very grateful for the many friends, family, and ministries who have encouraged, prayed and "cheered us on" through the ongoing peaks and valleys of our life journey:

- Bible Study Fellowship
- Indian Rocks Baptist Church
- Growth in Faith Ministry
- Navigators Ministry
- Samaritan's Purse
- Word of Life

Individuals who meaningfully contributed to *Hope for the Hurting*:

- Dr. Charlie Martin, Pastor
- Linda Gilden, editor
- Les Stobe, editor
- Irene and (Jim) Byers, editors/publishers
- Karen and David Rigsby, editors/publishers
- Alane Pearce, publishing and layout assistance

TO ALL OUR FAITHFUL PRAYER PARTNERS
To God be the Glory!

Blessings,
Carolyn and Michael Reynolds

Carolyn and Michael Reynolds

About the Authors

Dr. Michael Reynolds, a dentist by trade, has a heart for the grieving and a passion to help heal the hurting. He has been published in several devotionals, including *Upper Room.*

Michael and Carolyn both have been certified as Chaplains for Samaritan's Purse. They have also each completed Bible Institute diplomas in Biblical studies at Moody Bible Institute. Together they published a devotional book, *Pathway Pearls*, and a worship CD, *Pathways to Peace.*

Carolyn Reynolds is a life purpose coach who partners with women who are at a change point in their lives and seeking God's direction. She has served in women's ministry for over 30 years teaching, training, and coaching. She was also the president of an inter-denominational ministry and a hostess on a weekly TV broadcast. Carolyn enjoys ministering to women while speaking at retreats and conferences. Carolyn is the author of many Bible studies and magazine articles.

Carolyn and Michael Reynolds live on Florida's West Coast. They have been active in church ministry for many years, and have served on mission trips to various countries including: Kenya, South Africa, Haiti, and St. Lucia.

They have two grown children who also reside in Florida with their families.

Carolyn and Michael have a heart for reaching out to those who may be experiencing difficult times and continue ministering to others through their writing, speaking and volunteering.

Notes

Notes

Urgent Prayers

Urgent Prayers

Three people I can call any time:

Name:

Phone:

Name:

Phone:

Name:

Phone:

Made in the USA
Columbia, SC
26 October 2024